HELP!

I'M GRIEVING

Rebecca Wigley

Consulting Editor: Dr Jim Winter

© Day One Publications 2022
First printed 2022

ISBN 978-1-84625-721-6

Published by Day One Publications
Ryelands Road, Leominster, HR6 8NZ
Tel 01568 613 740
North America Toll Free 888 329 6630
email—sales@dayone.co.uk
website—www.dayone.co.uk

The image on the cover and throughout this booklet is used
under licence from Shutterstock.com

Printed by 4edge Limited

CONTENTS

INTRODUCTION

By no means am I an expert on grief or loss. I am a child of God who has suffered some losses and I feel led to share a little of my experiences. Everyone's experience of bereavement and loss is different. I know that we all 'cope' in different ways and face different temptations and struggles as we are called to travel this path. In no way is what I have written the rule of grief but I am sure it is not the exception.

When reading the other day in Mark's Gospel about the storm on Galilee, something jumped out at me that I had not seen before:

> *And when they had sent away the multitude, they took him even as he was in the ship. And there were also with him other little ships.'*
>   *(Mark 4:36)*

It was the phrase 'and there were also with him other little ships'. It seems strange to me that Mark, who is quite often brief in his accounts, saw fit to mention the other little ships. It frequently feels like we are little ships tossed about in the storms of life and we feel alone and often lost; but, as we have it written here, those little ships were with our Lord. The Lord, who stilled the storm with a word, still cares for his little ships today and he loves and cares for his people. Even though we change, God never changes. May we be like those little ships in our life storms—with the Lord Jesus.

Forgiveness of sins

I had the great privilege of being brought up in a loving Christian home and was taught Bible stories and the way of salvation from a babe in arms. I think I could have said all the right things to anyone who asked me without my truly knowing the Lord Jesus Christ personally.

When I was about sixteen years old, I had an argument with my Mum and I was pretty horrible to her. It was then, for the first time, I remember truly realising that I was not only sinning against my Mum, but also against God. I personally needed forgiveness of my sins. On a dark winter's evening I remember hanging off our bunk-bed and sobbing and asking the Lord to forgive me for being such a horrible person and sinning against him. I believe this was the beginning of my walk with the Lord and he opened my heart to show me my wretchedness, and also how forgiveness can be found in him if we trust in the Lord Jesus. One verse that is very special to me and always seems to pop up and be a blessing to me is from Isaiah:

> *Come now, and let us reason together,*
>   *saith the* LORD:
> *though your sins be as scarlet,*
>   *they shall be as white as snow;*
> *though they be red like crimson,*
>   *they shall be as wool.*   *(Isaiah 1:18)*

I urge you, if you do not know the forgiveness of your sins or you are not interested in the things of God, to ask the Lord to show you and help you. There is nothing more important in the whole of your life than to know the forgiveness of your sins. None of us knows when our last day on this earth will be, but we will all face death (unless the Lord first comes again) and eternity.

> *I love them that love me:*
>   *and those that seek me early shall find me.*
>   *(Proverbs 8:17)*

As for me, I know that I am nothing without my Saviour and that I need to return to the Lord to ask forgiveness for my sins daily. It is God's wonderful grace that keeps me and upholds me every day and God's gift of faith that allows me to rest in him.

No sympathy, please

Below is a brief outline of our losses, just so you are aware of whom I am mentioning in the pages that follow.

We lost our son Daniel in 2010, when he was 6 weeks and 6 days old. Early on in my pregnancy the doctors realised there was something wrong with Daniel, but they were not sure what the problem was. Daniel was born a huge 10 lb baby and he was soon diagnosed with a heart condition that was treated with medication. We were told he would likely grow out of it, but there was a small possibility that he might suddenly pass away.

Daniel had a cardiac arrest when I was out shopping with him and our daughter Kezia who was two at the time. Thankfully the ambulance arrived very quickly and I had only just begun to try a couple of breaths to keep him alive when they arrived. The staff at the hospital were able to get his heart briefly started but

I believe he went home to glory on the pavement outside the shop. Steve (my husband) made it to the hospital just as they announced that Daniel had died.

Soon after this a good family friend passed away fairly quickly after a short illness. I also had the privilege of being present when my maternal grandfather went home to glory.

Steve lost his grandmother who was in her nineties.

More recently, in 2018 my sister and best friend Deb passed away at the age of 27 after a four-year battle with cancer. Deb's husband Mash, along with the rest of the family, were very privileged to be with her as she drew her last breath and went home to her Saviour.

In 2020 amidst the COVID pandemic my paternal grandfather passed away of causes unrelated to COVID.

We have also lost a number of close family friends.

Not all grief is a bereavement

Something I want to mention early on is that there are many types of grief. Not all grief is a result of the death of someone close. The other day I was talking to a friend and we were trying to identify different types of 'grief', and there were too many to name. I cannot imagine the pain of not being able to have children, or the pain of a child that is far from the Lord. Before my sister was converted we lost contact with her for about a year and sometimes we did not even know where she was. This was an immense trial to my parents and we all grieved. The path of singleness can be a grief to bear, as can a long term illness, missed opportunities or personal mistakes, pain, loss of property or having something sentimental stolen—and there are many more examples. I am sure we all have different things in our lives that we have grieved over and probably continue to grieve over. The most important thing that we should all grieve over is, of course, our sins. We should not rest until we know the forgiveness of our sins. I pray that we all may have the assurance of having our sins forgiven.

Many times people have said to me when they have mentioned their personal trials and griefs, 'Oh, but we have not been through anything like you have in our lives.' I often think, 'On the other hand, there are many people who have dreadful trials, a lot worse than we have ever been through.' You can always find someone worse off than yourself. I try to politely disagree, because whatever you are going through at that moment, it is a trial and grief to you whether it is a seemingly small thing or a big trial. When you are in trials, they are bad and difficult and it is the way the Lord is seeing fit to walk you through.

I have often felt guilty for grieving or feeling down and sad. Sometimes we put on a brave face. Sometimes we show the British stiff upper lip, or we hide our grief because it is hard to deal with other people's reactions to it. Also, we do have so much to be thankful for that it sometimes feels wrong to grieve. All I can say is that the Lord Jesus mourned and wept over the grave of Lazarus, and so I think it is all right to feel sad and to grieve. If we have the

13

privilege of mourning, then it means we have had the privilege of being able to love.

> *Casting all your care upon him;*
> *for he careth for you.* *(1 Peter 5:7)*

Everyone grieves differently

This is pretty obvious, but it is true. The path we are called to walk is unique to us, even if sometimes the circumstances are very similar to, or even the same as, other people's. We all feel things differently and cope in different ways.

Some people are really quiet, others like to talk. I do think that men and women definitely grieve differently. It is in men's nature to try and fix things. This was true for Steve and me when we lost Daniel. Steve was very quiet and I wanted to talk. Steve had his work to keep his mind busy and I was at home feeling pretty dreadful at times. Our daughter Kezia was such a blessing to us both to keep us going. I think I cried pretty soon after Daniel died—a real gut-wrenching crying that breaks your heart in two. It is not a cleansing cry, but a painful cry, a cry that is like no other. After Deb passed away it took me months to cry. I really didn't want to cry like I had with Daniel, so I hid my pain. Eventually it all came out though and it was just as painful. I can easily talk about Daniel, but I still find it hard to talk about how I feel about Deb not being here. It is still too hard for me to put into words.

I know my Mum started her grieving the moment Deb was diagnosed with cancer. When my Mum's father was getting old and started needing more care, Mum was grieving as she was caring for him. After Grandad passed away, Mum said she had done all her grieving before he died, and how could she now be sad when he was in glory and no longer old and frail? That is not to say she does not miss him.

So, we all have different paths and experiences that are unique to us. I am so thankful we have a never-changing heavenly Father who is the same yesterday, today and forever.

Death

When someone you loves dies, it is agonizing. To watch someone you love leave this world is a privilege, but it is also dreadful. It will change you for ever. With my grandparents, watching them slowly deteriorate over time was very sad, but it was completely different from watching someone young slowly die. We were there when Grandad passed away. I was almost scared of him as he wasn't comfortable until the very end. I remember leaving the home where he passed away and driving home like a mad thing. It was one of those dark, wet nights and I nearly crashed the car. I really don't recommend doing that!

Deb was ill for four years and over that time her body got weaker and weaker, although she did enjoy periods of 'good health' as she was told a few times that she was free of cancer. Only it came back again. To see someone you love so young and so weak slowly dying is indescribable. In Deb's last few days, she

17

became a skeleton as the cancer ravaged her body, and before the medication was properly sorted she had times of writhing around in agony. Towards the end she only said a few sentences and they were very precious. The odd squeeze of her hand was so special. One of the last things she said was to Dad, as he read one of her favourite passages to her from John 14 about the mansions in glory. She whispered, 'Nearly there.' One of the last things she said to me was, 'I love you, too.' I remember saying to her once, 'Can you feel the Lord Jesus near you?' and she said, 'Yes.' Towards the end, Deb was basically just a living corpse, Her body was alive, but she was so ill that she almost didn't look like our Deb. Deb's dear husband said, 'She is still beautiful though.' On a glorious spring morning without a cloud in the sky with her husband and family close by, I watched her last breath as she entered glory.

The few things that Deb was able to say are so precious, but not everyone gets to have a long period of being able to say goodbye or to be prepared, so to speak, as we had with Deb. We have just lost a family friend unexpectedly. He was suddenly taken while in his garden. There are many people who have lost loved ones young and old in accidents, even in war and other events where people are taken from this world without any warning. With Daniel it was so quick and traumatic with his heart suddenly stopping. It is just so distressing and nothing can prepare you for it. I was out shopping on my own with Kezia and Daniel—it was dreadful, but the Lord provided three strangers to help me in driving me to hospital. One even worked at the hospital and was able to sort out my parking, etc. One thing that helped my healing with this was going back to the shop where Daniel passed away. I really did not want to, but felt I ought to, to help me in dealing with it. We have only been back once, but I prayed that I would be helped. I even found a dress in the shop that I still wear to this day.

However your loved one dies, this will stay with you for the rest of your days, and it is a tragic memory that will change you and impact you in ways that cannot be put into words. After Deb died it took me ages to not have my phone with me all the time as we were always on tenterhooks as to what would happen and if we were needed. All I can say is that time does help with the initial pain, but it never leaves you or goes away. Turn to the Lord Jesus who knows exactly how you feel and knows your pain and heartache.

Lost and bewildered

After the death of someone there is so much to sort out and it is often a confusing and bewildering experience, especially if you have never done anything like that before. I remember Steve and I going to the hospital to pick up Daniels's death certificate and sitting in some small room trying to be polite. The icing on the cake was the lady who handed me the clothes in which Daniel had died. I refused to take them, but she insisted that she had to give them to us. I told her to put them in the bin, but she said she had to give them to us. I remember Steve quietly took them and hid them from me. Poor lady, she was only doing her job. We then had to go and register Daniel's death where just a few weeks before Steve had registered his birth—no words can describe how I felt.

Then there was the visit to the undertakers to arrange the funeral. They were very kind and even made sure Daniel's coffin was wooden, as I did not want a white one that they normally used for babies. I think one of the hardest things was sorting out the clothes for Daniel to be buried in. I remember rummaging in the airing cupboard trying to find a particular babygro and making sure he had a nappy too! Daniels's burial and thanksgiving service was the first funeral I had ever been to.

When both grandfathers passed away my parents went through a lot of stress with probate and organising funerals. My Dad's father passed away in lockdown, so it was doubly stressful trying to get hold of the right people to sort things out. Things seemed to be twice as hard than in normal times. We could only have a small burial service due to the COVID restrictions.

Then there was the sorting out of the personal items of our loved ones. I shall never forget Mum and I helping Mash sort out Deb's belongings—it felt so intrusive, but it needed to be done. Everyone is different in this. Some people want it sorted straight away; others like to wait. There is no right or wrong way. We took most of Deb's clothes to a charity shop. Deb loved her clothes and over the years she had accumulated quite a bit. A lot of them were nice clothes, even some designer ones. They were lovely clothes from a beautiful young person. It was so hard going into the charity shop to give them all away. I do not think the ladies that volunteered in the shop knew what to make of all these amazing clothes that Mash and I were piling in. One of them started moaning about the hangers as a lot of the clothes were still on their hangers. I turned to her and said, 'Just take them, please.' She was about to argue, but I think the penny dropped when she took one look at my face, and she just said, 'OK!' I remember Mash opening up a big industrial size bin outside the charity shop and slinging in some loose hangers. We can smile about it now, but at the time it was such a hard thing to do.

Sorting out all the baby things that we no longer needed was tough. You know how much stuff you have with a newborn. I shall never forget my father-in-law helping me to take the pushchair and car seat fixtures out of the car. We gave away the nappies and milk to someone at church who had just had a baby. We had so many new clothes that friends and family had kindly given us, though they were just bundled up in the loft. We went through them some time later and gave them to charity. I have what I call a treasure box of a few things of Daniel's that I kept in the loft. I think I have looked at it only a couple of times. It sounds silly, but I cannot part with those items.

Mum and Dad had to help close up both of their parents' houses and help sort out all the stuff from them. It makes you realise how much rubbish we have and, really, a lot of it is worthless,. 'All is vanity', as Solomon wisely said.

I remember, about the time when Daniel would have been turning one, we were having to attend to his gravestone. I really did feel so sad and probably a bit bitter that we were sorting out his gravestone when we might have been celebrating his first birthday.

After the death of someone there is a lot to organise and so much to do that it is often after things begin to calm down and go back to a new 'normal' that the pain really starts to kick in. For then we are no longer engrossed in all the busyness. It is often then that you need the most help and support from others to know you are not forgotten. I used to think, 'If only I could run away from it all,' and I often think of David's Psalm 55 where he talks about being a dove flying away and escaping from the storm and tempest. Yet we know, as David says, that he did not want to be away from his God. Later on in the psalm he says:

> *Cast thy burden upon the LORD,*
>   *and he shall sustain thee:*
> *he shall never suffer the righteous to be moved*
>   *(Psalm 55:22)*

Precious

After Daniel passed away, my Dad wrote a piece about his thoughts and experiences of losing a grandson. Here is an excerpt from it:

> *Our moments spent with Daniel were*
> *very precious, but we know he was more*
> *precious to our Lord (Psalm 139:14–18).*
> *As he was in the womb he was not hid from*
> *the Lord, he saw all Daniel's substance. The*
> *Lord's thoughts towards him were precious.*
>
> *How precious also are thy thoughts unto me,*
>   *O God!*
>   *how great is the sum of them!*
>   *(Psalm 139:17)*
>
> *Daniel was redeemed by the precious*
> *blood of Christ (1 Peter 1:18–19). The*

events around his death, even though very
harrowing, were under the eye of God.
For we know that Daniel's death was also
precious to the Lord, for we read:

Precious in the sight of the LORD
  is the death of his saints.   (Psalm 116:15)

I do believe that Daniel is with the Lord,
which is far better, and that he was 'taken
away from the from the evil to come'
(Isaiah 57:1).

Why has all this happened? 1 Peter 1:7
speaks of 'the trial of your faith, being
much more precious than of gold'. May God
give us the grace to see and feel this in all
things.

But our God is in the heavens:
  he hath done whatsoever he hath pleased.
                                    (Psalm 115:3)

I remember that at Deb's funeral someone came up to
me a couple of times and quoted Psalm 116:15, that my
Dad mentioned above. At the time it did not really

mean too much to me, but since then it has come back to me many times. However painful our loved one's death is to us on this earth, if they are one of the Lord's then their death is precious to him and they are very precious to the Lord. What a comfort this is to those who are left behind!

Grief is a funny thing!

Yy ou might say, 'What a strange title to a chapter—it certainly doesn't make sense or seem at all right.' Well, in my experience it can be 'funny' in a few ways. It is funny because grief can creep up on you—you can be sailing along thinking all is well and you are doing all right, and, *bam*, it hits you right in the stomach. An overwhelming wave of sadness and pain envelops you. Your eyes well up and your heart almost stops. This has happened many, many times with me and it does not seem to get any better. Quite often it comes at the most inappropriate of times and I either squash it down to bury the pain, or floods of tears just erupt. One time a friend was pregnant and I was not aware of this wonderful news. We were at a big function and there were a lot of people there. Someone came up to me, almost certain that I did not know, to inform me with great delight that this mutual friend was pregnant. Thankfully I was able to smile and say how wonderful it was, but inside I was breaking. As I walked away, tears just streamed out; I was a mess and simply could not control myself. It was near the end of the function and thankfully we were able to leave early. I sobbed all the way home.

The Lord taught me through this incident. I was relying on my own strength and I remember thinking, as the person spoke to me, 'Lord, you got me into this situation: so you sort it out!' It was prideful and arrogant on my part. The attitude behind my prayer was full of pride and anger. I really had to humble myself again and ask for forgiveness before the Lord and look to him in humility, not pride, for his continuing help and grace.

Grief can literally be funny—there is often a fine line between tears and laughter. Very often when we were children and we were in hysterical laughter, my Mum would say, 'You will be crying in a minute,' and quite often we were! I frequently find myself turning into my Mum and saying this to our daughter. Not many people know this, and I am almost reluctant to share it, but at my sister's burial I nearly had a hysterical moment. I was absolutely filled with dread before her burial, the memories of Daniel's grave-side service still haunting me. To this day I know it is tradition to look in the grave and put some dirt on the casket, but after looking at Daniel's tiny box in the earth at the bottom of the hole I cannot bring myself to do this at other grave-side services. Steve and I very frequently quietly walk away after the grave-side service has finished. Anyway, going back to Deb's burial, the dread of watching Mum and Dad and Mash (Deb's husband) and the wider family go through this ordeal was awful. The Lord, however, upheld us in a remarkable way. We were all solemnly standing round the grave while the service was in progress, and suddenly there was a rustling and commotion in the bushes, just behind the minister's feet. Lo and behold, there were two moles, of all things—let us just say up to no good! Now this is just the thing that Deb and I would find absolutely hilarious and very often we would be in stitches at silly things like this. All I could think of was Deb sitting up in the casket catching my eye and saying, 'Can you see that?' and flopping back down again! I could barely keep it together at the time, and the funny thing was no one else noticed it! To this day I believe the Lord sent this funny incident to help me through such a hard and devastating moment. God is in control of all things. We read in 1 Kings 17 how God commanded the ravens to feed Elijah—God never changes and he is still the same God today and he will use whatever he sees fit.

I remember not long after Daniel passed away, that we were walking up the path to our house, and Kezia was toddling along in front of Steve and me. She did something funny and we both burst out laughing—and we instantly felt guilty at laughing so soon after losing Daniel. Do not feel guilty for smiling or laughing through your losses—those who have gone would want you to enjoy the small happiness that occurs on this earth. Most importantly, remember that however much we go through, if we are true children of God, nothing can take away that true joy of the saving love of the Lord Jesus. We certainly do not feel joyful when we are grieving, but we must not base our joy and eternal life on how we feel. Joy is a God-given gift. Keep turning to the Lord and ask him to show, renew and preserve your joy in him.

And ye now therefore have sorrow: but I will see you again, and your heart shall rejoice, and your joy no man taketh from you.'
(John 16:22)

Thankful for grief

Yes, another strange heading for a chapter— but with God's help I am able to say that I am thankful that he has let me feel this pain and anguish. It is certainly not easy to say this and it is not flippantly said. It is a constant learning process with me, to be thankful with a continual ebbing and flowing and always needing the Lord to help me in this. Also, being thankful is not in any way making light of what we have been through and in no way is it suggesting that the path we have trodden and are still treading has not been and does not remain hard, because some days it is still complete agony.

After Daniel passed away a very kind Christian neighbour who had lost a baby through stillbirth many years ago, came and visited us and she said, 'One day you will be thankful to God for allowing this to happen.' I thought she was completely off her rocker at the time, but her comment has often come back to me through the loss of Daniel and my sister Deb. Through the help of the Lord I am able to say that I am thankful in many different ways.

I am so thankful that people have been saved, especially through my sister Deb's amazing testimony that she was able to share—what is more important than eternal life?

To be at the deathbed of a believer is a precious thing and it is a privilege to be there. Deb was so sure of her eternal home, and to hear her speak of her Saviour was wonderful.

I am thankful to be given the strength and grace to continue, to truly know that I am nothing without the Lord Jesus.

I am so thankful that Steve and I are truly able to be empathetic and understand a little of what others are going through. The Lord has brought so many people into our lives in the most unexpected ways—people who are going through, or have been through, similar losses. To be able to be of some small comfort to others makes our losses so much easier to bear.

One lady who was led across our path had, like us, been told that there was something wrong with her baby and she was advised to have an abortion. I remember talking to her the day before she was due to have the abortion and was able to tell her of how we were helped in our situation with Daniel. The next day I heard that she had not gone through with the abortion and had decided to carry on with the pregnancy, come what may. It was at the time that Daniel passed away that she gave birth to a perfectly healthy little girl. It was such a precious moment to hold that beautiful little girl. We have lost touch with them now, but I often pray for that little girl and wonder what plan the Lord has for her life.

> *And he said unto me, My grace is sufficient for thee: for my strength is made perfect in weakness. Most gladly therefore will I rather glory in my infirmities, that the power of Christ may rest upon me.*
>
> *(2 Corinthians 12:9)*

It is very true that when you go through deep trials and pains, God does this to bring you closer to him. The presence of the Lord during these times can be so wonderful and I have been blessed when I have felt his closeness.

When Daniel passed away outside the shop was one of those times. It is indescribable how at peace I felt and that I could almost feel the Lord's presence. In looking back, I am so thankful for his nearness and presence, it was so amazing. Another time was when my sister was nearing the end of her life. I was at such a low point and the Lord made a verse from Genesis very special to me:

> *But the dove found no rest for the sole of her foot, and she returned unto him into the ark, for the waters were on the face of the whole earth: then he put forth his hand, and took her, and pulled her in unto him into the ark.*
> *(Genesis 8:9)*

It spoke to me that Deb's work on this earth was done and God was calling her home. She was one of God's children and he was drawing her home.

The times that you really feel the Lord speaking to you are so wonderful and treasured that they remain with you for ever, and again it makes the trial you are going through a little sweeter.

Memories

What a blessing the memories of our loved ones are! If we are able to look at the photos of our family and friends who are no longer with us, the memories are so precious. I know not everyone wants to see photos—the memories they arouse are too painful. The night before Daniel died I was so tired that Steve did all of the night-time feeds for the first time. That morning, Steve was late to work as Daniel was lying on our bed smiling and almost talking, as babies do. Steve was able to spend precious time with Daniel and take lots of photos, not knowing it would be the last time he would see him alive. He is so thankful for those special memories with him. I spent most of my life, when I was living at home, sharing a bedroom with Deb. We used to argue and bicker a lot, but, looking back, I'm thankful for those memories. I wish I had been more thankful at the time and wish I had not taken things for granted so much!

I'm sure we all have regrets about our previous actions and feel bad about past mistakes—things we wish we had not said, or bad thoughts that we had entertained about our lost ones. I have many, many regrets, too many to name, some too dreadful to speak of, and it is a separate grief all on its own to remember and grieve over these, to wish I had not done this, or said that, or reacted in such a way. All I can say is, take it to the Lord in prayer. He knows how frail and weak we are—we are but dust, but we have a wonderful Saviour who is waiting to forgive.

Missing

Missing really is an inadequate word to describe the feeling of missing someone after they have died. The utter desperation that suddenly comes across you when you realise time and time again that you will never see them again on this earth. I miss Daniel so much that my heart aches. It took me months to not turn around in the car and check he was all right in his car seat, even though we only had him a short time. My grandmother says that she turns to talk to Grandad and suddenly realises that he is no longer there. When the three of us go out, we can never buy a family ticket as it is not worth the value of just paying for two adults and a child. A lot of things are set up for a family of four and very often we sit looking at an empty chair, always knowing there is someone missing. I think where Daniel is concerned I probably miss him more now as time goes on, thinking of what could have been rather than what is. Recently it would have been his birthday and he would have been 10, and I wonder what he would have looked like.

I cannot imagine how it must feel to lose a husband and companion. For Mash to become a widower at such a young age was truly dreadful. For those who have lost their spouse after many years of marriage it must be something they cannot get over, and the words 'missing them' just really doesn't touch it.

With my granddads, I miss them and their funny quirks and sayings. Only the other day I was teaching Kezia a silly rhyme that Grandad used to sing! There are a couple of good family friends we have lost over the years, that I really miss. One of them lived close to us and he was always popping over with something or just to say hello—I just miss him.

I miss my sister so much that I can hardly talk about it. She was my best friend: the type of friend you could be with and say what you think; the type of friend with whom often no words were needed. I can no longer speak to her, or have a giggle with her.

We, as a family, talk about our lost loved ones quite a bit. We bring them into conversation a lot and remember how they were, or imagine what they would have said. Our daughter, Kezia, is sometimes the spitting image of Deb in the things she says and in her mannerisms. Deb used to sneak off to the toilet just as there was any washing or drying up to be done, and when Kezia does similar things, we have a saying in our house, 'You're doing an Auntie Deb!'

There are constant reminders in our lives of our loved ones and I know I find it varies from day to day how we are able to deal with missing them. Very often it is in the quietness of our hearts when we feel the most aching and longing to see them again. It is a reminder to me that this is not our home and all things are fleeting, but, on the other hand, we do have so much to be thankful for.

Anniversaries and birthdays

The birthdays of our loved ones are very hard and, for me, they are just tough days to get through. I quite often want to be quiet on their birthdays, but I am sure other people are different and want to do something special.

I know there can be many anniversary days—from remembering the day of their death, to wedding anniversaries, to special days that mean something only to you. Very often no one else will remember these dates and it can be hard. We have a couple of friends who individually remember Daniel's and Deb's day of death. They both, every year, send us some flowers—it is so kind and so nice to know someone remembers.

I think also that everyone is different and I think it is especially different for men. I do not think they particularly remember dates like women do, but you can be sure that just because they do not remember the dates it does not mean that they feel their loss in any lesser way. I was speaking to someone the other day and he said he did not particularly remember birthdays and anniversaries, but he just felt the grief every day.

On the other hand, as time goes on we may often forget and not think of our loved ones, and I remember feeling guilty for not thinking about Daniel. For me, though, I think this is all part of the healing process. More importantly, we often forget our heavenly Father—how often in our daily lives we do not turn to the Lord, or even remember him as we go about our day. It is good to be reminded that even though we forget our Lord, God will not forget us.

> *Can a woman forget her sucking child,*
> *that she should not have compassion on*
> *the son of her womb?*
> *yea, they may forget,*
> *yet will I not forget thee.'*   (Isaiah 49:15)

Nightmares and night watches

For months after the deaths of Daniel and Deb (mostly after Deb passed away) I had the most dreadful nightmares. They were either re-living different things that had happened, or dreams of completely random things that involved Deb being alive again. Apparently, I was making strange noises in my sleep and occasionally I would wake up screaming in a cold sweat. Steve said that after Daniel died I would cry in my sleep. I can only speak of my experience, and everyone is different—but for me I think it was my brain processing everything and probably a bit of post-traumatic stress disorder.

To be unable to sleep properly, and when you do to have nightmares, is not pleasant. Occasionally something will happen, almost a trigger, and I will still have bad dreams. The number of nights I have spent lying awake are too many to count, but is it not wonderful that the Lord never sleeps? He is always watching over us.

I have tried to follow the verse in Psalm 63:6,

When I remember thee upon my bed,
and meditate on thee in the night watches.

I try to spend my sleepless times praying for people the Lord brings to mind. Although many, many times I fail and read a book or waste time on my phone or go downstairs for a cup of tea and a bowl of cereal, I am so thankful for the Lord's help and presence. It makes me realise what a gift sleep is and something we should not take for granted. We should ask God to give us sleep. I know of some people who, after losses, do not generally suffer with nightmares or dreams, but do suffer with getting to sleep and end up going to bed very late. Many times God seems so very far away and I feel so alone, especially through the frustrations of bad dreams and sleepless nights. Yet I would do well to remember God's word, for he will keep me, and he watches over us as we sleep, and give us sleep.

'Behold, he that keepeth Israel
shall neither slumber nor sleep.'
(Psalm 121:4)

Grief is lonely

It has often been said that you can be the most lonely in a room full of people—this is so true when you are grieving, in my experience. Countless times during my own walk I have felt so alone and misunderstood and almost shunned. Old friends will often not know what to say, or unintentionally will say hurtful things, and many times you have to grin and bear it, smiling through a conversation when inside you are falling apart. It feels like old wounds are being opened up again, with salt being poured in and rubbed in for good measure! I am so thankful that I have a friend that 'sticketh closer than a brother' and 'he knoweth our frame and remembers that we are dust'. The Lord knows what we are going through and he truly does understand. It is so wonderful that he can see and know exactly how we feel.

Church, unfortunately, has sometimes been one of the worst places where I have felt so alone. I remember one time not long after Daniel had passed away when I attended a midweek service. Steve had rushed home from work and I then rushed out of the door to drive to church, a forty minute drive away. I was late, I struggled to find a parking space, and somehow managed to tread in dog muck between the car and the church. I sank down in the pew and the unpleasant aroma wafted up. I was in a foul mood, and, lo and behold, our pastor preached from Psalm 127, especially focusing in on the blessings of men having a quiver full of children! You can imagine how I felt, having just lost our son and been in a rush trying to get to church. I barely held it together and slipped out quickly at the end ... I felt so alone.

I remember that after Deb passed away going back to church was really hard. We had been away as we had been living at the hospice with Deb for her last days, and the thought of having to deal with people's sympathetic glances and kind words was almost too much to bear. Although everyone was very kind, I just didn't want to talk to anyone—we slipped in late and left in the last hymn so that we did not have to do so.

I often find weddings very hard, also family gatherings ... seeing sisters enjoying special days together, wishing my sister Deb was still with us ... and don't talk about family photos! I am sure you can imagine how I must feel. In all these things I have to be reminded once again to be thankful for all the riches that I do have and to be thankful that I have known what it is to have a sister and son.

> *There is a friend that sticketh closer than a brother.* (Proverbs 18:24)

Hope, the dog

When my sister was ill we decided to get a family dog to help our daughter through it all. Steve had been brought up with dogs and had always wanted one. I, on the other hand, was not particularly keen, but thought, 'Why not? Let's get one!'

So we got this lovely little Cavalier King Charles puppy and Kezia loved her so much. My Dad chose the name 'Hope' as it seemed so appropriate at the time. Hope was a little comfort dog and loved to curl up on anyone's lap that was free, or she seemed to sense if you were down and was ready to snuggle up to whoever needed it! Hope even spent a lot of time at the hospice in Deb's final days. Just over a year ago she suddenly became very ill and we had to make the difficult decision to have her put to sleep. Now, I am not a dog person at all, but I tell you these animals get right under your skin, and if any of you have been through the loss of an animal you will know it is tough. They do become part of the family, and to have to make the decision to have them put down is so, so hard. It was dreadful for Kezia: she had not just lost her pet, she had lost her little friend. Kezia was off school in lockdown and she heard Steve and me talking to the vet, and unfortunately was around when we had to make the decision to have Hope put down. It was absolutely awful. I think Kezia cried for a whole day. It was almost as though she was also grieving for Deb. We could do nothing to help her. Kezia was beside herself and angry too. It seemed to her that the answers to her prayers were quite often 'no'. My Dad came over, despite the lockdown rules, and took her for a walk to try and help her. You could not make it up, could you?!

For us, the only thing we could do was to get another puppy. We wrestled over this as we did not want to spoil Kezia, but it felt, for us, that it was one of those heartaches in Kezia's life that we could fix in some small way. Amazingly, Steve had saved up some money for expenses and we had just the right amount to buy a new puppy. So a week later we made a dodgy lockdown trip to the border of Wales to pick up this tiny puppy we call Smudge. I wish you could see the photo of Kezia sitting in the back of the car with her new little friend!

It has often been a burden for me about what others might be thinking, and it is something I struggle with. We have a little caravan in which we take quite a few holidays in order to get away and have a time of rest. For us it is a way of coping with the deaths of Daniel and Deb. I often worry what others think of our going away quite a lot, but they are simple holidays, and the rest and change does us and our marriage so much good. So when we bought an expensive dog in lockdown straight after losing Hope, it bothered me what others might think, which I know is so silly. It is something I have to turn to the Lord about, and not worry about others' opinions. Grief has taught me not to judge others as well, for often we do not know people's circumstances and situations. Very often we get only a small idealised glimpse into their lives and we do not have a clue about what different things people are struggling with and the anguish that is sometimes behind the veneer we all put up.

Grief and anger

Now, for me, this is especially difficult. To say that I have not been angry would be a lie. I have felt such bitterness and anger. To my shame, I have even felt anger at God. I have always had a fiery temper and it is a constant battle within me. A friend once tore me off a strip when I cautiously admitted to feeling angry. This friend said it was wrong to feel angry and that I must not be angry. Unfortunately, I was angry and felt angry, and if I am honest I have been many times since. I know it is wrong to be angry and it is a sin that needs to be repented of. I really did not need my friend telling me off for something I knew was wrong and was already struggling with.

Someone once said to me, 'Tell God how you feel.' This has been such a help to me over the years and still is. Such simple words, but, oh, how hard it is for me! To openly admit to God in prayer that I was angry with him and with the various situations is frightening, even though God already knows exactly what is going on in my heart. It took me a while, but once I told God exactly how I felt and confessed my sins, it was like a burden being lifted. Anger and bitterness are sins and to carry them around is nothing but stupid. I have to constantly ask God to protect me from these stumbling blocks in my life. God does give more grace and I can truly say that he has helped and continually does help me over my besetting sins.

If you, too, are struggling with anger, read some of David's Psalms (13, 22, 31). In some of them he is in despair and angry and he tells God exactly how he feels. It is always encouraging how often David puts in a 'But' after he has had a moan!

> *But I trusted in thee, O LORD:*
> *I said, Thou art my God.*   (Psalm 31:14)

May we be able to put our trust in God, for he does all things well.

Empty

During grief I have felt so empty and lost that I have had no care for almost anything. I have struggled with my weight and, unfortunately, have an unhealthy habit of comfort eating. To this day it is a constant battle for me. During and after different phases of grief I have also not had the desire to eat, and so I have experienced both sides of the coin, so to speak! I remember being unable to prepare meals after Deb died. It was such a struggle to think about such mundane things that we ended up just eating easy, unhealthy things, which was not good. I think the feeling of emptiness is a continual problem, but it is the Lord's way of bringing us to a point where we realise that this world has nothing to offer. I believe it is the Lord's way of refining us and drawing us closer to him—all of him and none of me.

The days after a loved one has passed away are particularly hard as things return to 'normal'. It feels like you are forgotten and everyone else gets on with their lives while you are continuing in your grief.

For me, this was when I often felt the lowest. It was particularly hard after Daniel died—I had lost my baby and my body was aching to hold him and care for my baby. I had empty, aching arms. I used to pray that I would be able just to hold him one more time and feel the softness of his head on my cheek. We lived quite far away from family and Steve had his escape in work and was often working long hours, out on out-of-hours calls. Kezia and I struggled on (this is not to say Steve was not struggling too). We would go for long walks round the village where we lived and Kezia kept me entertained with her lively character. She was, and is, such a blessing to us. When we were having bad days, I would say to Kezia, 'Come on, let's sing.' We would tearfully sing the chorus:

Trust and obey,
For there is no other way
To be happy in Jesus,
But to trust and obey.

It was all we could get out through our tears, but we just wanted to trust in our Lord who knows best and does all things well.

I remember after Deb passed away feeling incredibly hollow and empty. As a family we had all (especially Mash, Deb's husband, who had taken time off work to be with Deb in her last days) been incredibly busy travelling two hours each way to visit Deb, taking her to appointments, often in London, and spending time with her as she had treatment. As previously mentioned, we lived in the hospice with Deb for her final few days. After all this, returning to 'normal' life after her funeral was so strange and we had almost no purpose because all we were left with were memories and empty, broken hearts.

On a side note, my prayer mentioned above about wishing I could hold Daniel one last time and feel that softness of his head on my cheek has, in a way, been answered. Many friends and relatives have had babies and I have been able to hold them and rejoice at the wonder of new life, all with the help and grace given to me by God. My brother and sister-in-law recently had a precious son, and a couple of times I have had the privilege of being able to hold him up to my check while he slept. That soft baby feel and smell is the best thing and I cried as I held that special nephew, knowing that God answers prayers.

Watching others go through grief

I think one of the hardest things is to watch others go through loss. Watching my Mum and Dad lose their daughter was so hard, seeing them go through agonies and having their hearts broken; watching my Dad weep and become a broken man, all the while knowing I was grieving myself and losing my sister, but also knowing in a small way how he felt; helping our daughter through the loss of her dear Auntie whom she loved so, so much and holding her as she sobbed; seeing Deb's husband go through unmentionable agonies that only those who have lost a spouse can truly enter into; seeing my older brother cry by Deb's grave and almost become older overnight; watching your husband being unable to fix things and become silent in his pain.

It is hard to know what to say and do when you see others grieve—everyone is different. Even after all we have lost, I still struggle to know what to say to others walking this path. I have found that so many people do not say anything—they almost avoid you. Others have a lot to say which sometimes is not helpful! After Deb died people kept saying to me, 'At least you know where she is.' I think I could have screamed at them! I knew where she was and I didn't need anyone else to tell me that! It was no help to me in the current pain and loss I was feeling!

When you are grieving it is often the small gestures that mean so much, the squeeze on your arm as someone walks by; the bunch of flowers quietly given on anniversary dates; the, 'How are you really doing?'; the offer of a coffee; the meal delivered; the simple card saying you are being prayed for. All of these things are such a blessing.

From our experiences, I feel that it is better to say something to someone who is grieving than not to say anything at all. Mention their loved one by name. I love it when someone mentions Deb's and Daniel's names. Do not be afraid to ask questions—it is very often what the bereaved person needs.

One thing I have found very hurtful is when people withhold news from you after a painful loss, especially good news. For us, particularly, it has been when a friend or family member is expecting a baby. When people have not told us, it is very, very hard to hear it second-hand. Sometimes we have only heard just before the baby is born, or even after the baby is born. I think people are afraid of causing more pain. All I would say is, maybe send a text to let them know, or a quick phone call before you meet up, to give the person time to process and grieve in private. I have some good friends who always send me a text when they are expecting and it gives me time to grieve for us, but then rejoice with them at the wonder and blessing of new life. Yes, it does hurt—but in no way does it detract from the joy and happiness.

At the end of the day, God is the only one who knows how we truly feel, and he knows exactly what is going on in the darkest places of our hearts and he can and will comfort us in our losses. Prayer is hard, but the Lord knows, and he is the God of all comfort,

> *who comforteth us in all our tribulation,*
> *that we may be able to comfort them*
> *which are in any trouble, by the comfort*
> *wherewith we ourselves are comforted of God.*
> *(2 Corinthians 1:4)*

It is well

It is true to say that I have sinned greatly through my grief and often not acted or behaved wisely, but I have a merciful and forgiving God who has helped and upheld me, and I can truly say that it is only by his grace that I continue to this day. God mercifully takes away my anger and bitterness and gives me grace for each day, hour and minute.

In the hours after Daniel died, our pastor and his wife came to the hospital and afterwards to our home, and before they left he read and prayed, choosing a passage in 2 Kings 4 about the lady whose son had just died. Elisha came up to the house and asked if all was well, and even though her son had died she replied, 'It is well.' I remember having mixed emotions as our pastor read this passage. I felt like punching him and shouting out, 'Of course she said it is well when her son was going to be raised to life again—don't you realise our son is dead?' The other half of me was praying, 'Lord, grant me grace to be able to say "It is well."' Thankfully, I kept my peace and no violence erupted from me! The Lord has graciously answered my many prayers on this and has enabled me to say, 'It *is* well.' I used to sing to myself the hymn that Horatio Spafford wrote (*When peace like a river*) after he lost his children at sea. It truly is well; the Lord had taken Daniel home to be with him. My prayers that the Lord would save him had been answered and he is with his Saviour for all eternity.

We were able to have this hymn at Daniel's thanksgiving service, Deb and her husband chose it for their wedding and later for Deb's funeral service, and Steve had it at his baptism. This hymn, in a way, has become our family's hymn as we have all been able to say, with the Lord's help, 'It is well.'

> *Run now, I pray thee, to meet her, and say*
> *unto her, Is it well with thee? is it well with*
> *thy husband? is it well with the child? And*
> *she answered, It is well.*　　　*2 Kings 4:26*

In conclusion

There is so much more that could be said, and lots I am sure I have missed out, but I hope these few thoughts have been a help to you, although I guess many of you have thought, 'I don't feel like that,' or, 'That's a strange thing to say!' We are all fearfully and wonderfully made; we are all unique; so our grief journeys will also be unique, as the paths we are called to walk with the Lord are different.

Do excuse the ramblings and thoughts of a heartbroken woman. Yes, I do believe that losing someone does break your heart, and I often say to Steve, 'I'm not the same girl you married.' Loss does change you. I need to pray daily that the Lord will give me grace and that he will sustain me and keep me from being bitter. I remember early on after we lost Daniel I thought I was coping all right and was not bitter. I was out for a walk with Kezia when I saw a family come out of some flats with a baby, and I gave myself a pat on the back and thought, 'Well done, you are coping well, you don't feel bitter.' Then I gave a second look and the dad was holding a tiny baby, and, oh, the bitter thoughts and deep dislike towards that family came into my heart. It shook me to the core. I was shocked that I could feel like that and I was so ashamed. It was in that moment that the Lord showed me that I needed to rely on him for everything, that I need his grace to get though every moment of every day. There is that saying, 'a day at a time'. But we as a family often say that it is not a day at a time, it is often an hour, minute, or second at a time. I am so thankful that the Lord showed me how wretched I am and how I need him every hour. It is so wonderful to feel God's help and strength, for surely when we are weak then we are strong through him. It is only the Lord who keeps me and helps me through, for I truly am nothing without my Saviour.

God's grace truly is amazing and it is new every day. He gives us just what we need for that day, and neither more nor less, if we ask of him. One of the things the Lord has used to help prevent me from being bitter is that I help out at our church's toddler group. It often makes me smile that I, a girl who has lost her baby, is doing this work. I am sure the Lord has a good smile and it is only through him that I am able to do this.

Very often grief is felt just in the quietness of our broken hearts; only the Lord sees and knows, and I am thankful that no one else can see the blackness of my broken heart. As it says in the Psalms,

> *He healeth the broken in heart,*
> *and bindeth up their wounds. (Psalm 147:3)*

Ask God, and he will heal your broken heart.

Grief has taught me so many things and I am still learning. One of them is that we should live our lives in the view of eternity. I am sure that one look at our Lord Jesus' face and we will forget all the trials and tribulations in this world. This world is just passing; nothing is permanent and is fading away; we are only here for such a short while. There really is only one thing needful, and that is to know that your sins are forgiven. I pray that you too will know the Lord as your Saviour and that he will help you in your path of loss and grief and that you too will be helped to say, 'It is well.'

> *Surely he hath borne our griefs,*
> *and carried our sorrows.'* (Isaiah 53:4)

[You can read my sister's story in the book *A Silly Girl With A Silly Hat*. Available from Amazon and other good bookstores.]

Booklets in the *Help!* series include …

HELP—For the Bullied and the Bully (CHARLOTTE BUNGE)
ISBN 978-1-84625-672-1

HELP! How Can I Ever Forgive? (PAUL WILLIAMS)
ISBN 978-1-84625-527-4

HELP! I am Facing a Trial (JIM WINTER)
ISBN 978-1-84625-687-5

HELP! I am Walking Through Trauma (KATHERINE BEJIDE)
ISBN 978-1-84625-641-7

HELP! I Can't Submit to My Husband (GLENDA HOTTON)
ISBN 978-1-84625-321-8

HELP! I Cannot Cope With Change (JIM WINTER)
ISBN 978-1-84625-598-4

HELP! I Cannot Sleep (JIM WINTER)
ISBN 978-1-84625-716-2

HELP! I Feel Ashamed (SUE NICEWANDER)
ISBN 978-1-84625-320-1

HELP! I Have Breast Cancer (BRENDA FRIELDS)
ISBN 978-1-84625-216-7

HELP! I'm A Tired Parent (TOM PARKER)
ISBN 978-1-84625-712-4

HELP! I'm Caught Up In A Crisis (SIMON J ROBINSON)
ISBN 978-1-84625-691-2

HELP! I'm Confused about Credit and Debt (MARTIN SWEET)
ISBN 978-1-84625-526-7

HELP! I'm In Pain (DEBORAH SMITH)
ISBN 978-1-84625-619-6

HELP! I'm Living with Terminal Illness (REGGIE WEEMS)
ISBN 978-1-84625-319-5

HELP! I Need to Know about Narcissism (JOHN STELEY)
ISBN 978-1-84625-633-2

HELP! I Need to Make A Will (CHRIS HUGHES)
ISBN 978-1-84625-713-1

HELP! I Struggle with Anxiety (PHIL COTTRELL)
ISBN 978-1-84625-669-1

HELP! I've Been Deployed (RODDY MACLEOD)
ISBN 978-1-84625-459-8